D0835361

love letters

A selection of the most famous poetry
and prose of all time

Love Letters
© Summersdale Publishers 2005

Summersdale Publishers Ltd
46 West Street
Chichester
West Sussex
PO19 1RP
UK

Printed and bound in Great Britain

ISBN 1 84024 435 6

Acknowledgements

Letters still in copyright are taken from the following sources and reprinted by the kind permission of the following publishers, individuals and organisations:

A. P. Watt Ltd on behalf of Sophie Partridge and the Garnet Estate, *Carrington — Letters and Extracts from her Diary*

John Murray, from a letter by Byron

Disclaimer

contents

Romanticism is the art of presenting people with the Literary works which are capable of affording them the greatest possible pleasure, in the present state of their customs and beliefs.

Henri Beyle (called Stendhal)

verse

If ever two were one, then surely we.

If ever man were lov'd by wife, then thee;

If ever wife was happy in a man,

Compare with me ye women if you can.

I prize thy love more than whole mines of Gold,

Or all the riches that the east doth hold.

My love is such that rivers cannot quench,

Nor ought but love from thee, give recompense.

Thy love is such I can no way repay,

The heavens reward thee manifold repay.

Then while we live, in love let's so persevere,

That when we live no more, we may live ever.

Ann Bradstreet

She walks in beauty, like the night
Of cloudless climes and starry skies,
And all that's best of dark and bright
Meet in her aspect and her eyes;
Thus mellow'd to that tender light
Which heaven and gaudy day denies.

Lord Byron

Though **weary**,
love is not tired;
Though pressed, it is not straitened;
Though **alarmed**, it is not confounded,
Love securely passes through all.

Thomas A. Kempis

All love, at first, like **generous** wine,
Ferments and frets until 'tis fine,
But, when 'tis settled on the lee,
And from th' impurer matter **free**,
Becomes the richer still the older,
And proves the **pleasanter** the colder.

Samuel Butler

Deare, when I from thee am gone,
Gone are all my joyes at once;
I loved thee, and thee alone,
In whose love I joyed once.
And although your sights I leave,
Sight wherein my joyes do lie,
Till that death do sense bereave,
Never shall affection die.

John Dowland

Through all **Eternity** to thee
A joyful song I'll raise,
For oh! Eternity's too short
To utter all thy **Praise**.

Joseph Addison

Never so **happily** in one
Did **heaven** and earth combine;
And yet 'tis flesh and blood alone
That makes her so **divine**.

Thomas D'Urfey

O, my luve's like a red red rose
That's newly sprung in June:
O my luve's like a melodie
That's sweetly played in tune.

Robert Burns

I **love** thee, I love thee,
'Tis all that I can say;
It is my vision in the night,
My **dreaming** in the day.

Thomas Hood

What's in a **name**? That which we
call a rose
By any other name would
smell as **sweet**;
So Romeo would, were he not
Romeo called.

William Shakespeare

prose

The way you let your hand rest in mine, my bewitching sweetheart, fills me with happiness. It is the perfection of confiding love. Everything you do, the little unconscious things in particular, charms me and increases my sense of nearness to you, identification with you, till my heart is overflowing.

Woodrow Wilson

I cannot exist without you – I am forgetful of everything but seeing you again – my life seems to stop there – I see no further. You have absorb'd me. I have a sensation at the present moment as though I were dissolving – I have been astonished that men could die martyrs for religion – I have shudder'd at it – I shudder no more – I could be martyr'd for my religion – Love is my religion – I could die for that – I could die for you. My creed is Love and you are its only tenet – You have ravish'd me away by a power I cannot resist.

John Keats

Love is... born with the pleasure of looking at each other, it is fed with the necessity of seeing each other, it is concluded with the impossibility of separation.

Jose Marti Y Perez

Imagine two cars of the same make heading towards each other and they're gonna crash, head-on. Well, it's like one of those scenes from a film – they're doing a hundred miles an hour, they both slam their brakes on the floor and they stop just in the nick of time with their bumpers almost touching but not quite.

John Lennon's account of his first meeting with Yoko Ono

When she saw him, she felt a stab in her heart that persons who have never been dazed by love take for a metaphor.

Abel Hermant

The ideal story is that of two people who go into love step by step, with a fluttered consciousness, like a pair of children venturing together into a dark room.

Robert Louis Stevenson

The best and most beautiful things in the world cannot be seen or even touched. They must be felt by the heart.

Helen Keller

Romance cannot be put into quantity production – the moment love becomes casual, it becomes commonplace.

F. L. Allen

Falling in love had changed the landscape of her life, as an earthquake did.

Charlotte Lamb

So he was happy without a care in the world. A meal together, a walk along the highroad in the evening, a way she had of putting her hand to her hair, the sight of her straw hat hanging on the window latch, a great many things besides in which Charles had never thought to find pleasure, now made up the tenor of his happiness.

Gustave Flaubert

Love does not consist in gazing at each other but in looking in the same direction.

Antoine de Saint-Exupéry

There are times when love seems to be over... [but] these desert times are simply the way to the next oasis which is far more lush and beautiful after the desert crossing.

Madeleine L'Engle

I think we have come out on the other side meaning that we love each other more than we ever did when we loved each other most.

Archibald MacLeish on 60 years of marriage

Love is a desire that comes straight from the heart with a wealth of exceeding pleasure. Our eyes first give birth to love, and our hearts give it sustenance.

Jacopo da Lentino

one-liners

All **love** is sweet, **given**
or returned.

Percy Bysshe Shelley

Love distils **desire** upon the eyes,
love brings bewitching **grace**
into the **heart**.

Euripides

Two **souls** with but a single thought,

two **hearts** that beat as one.

John Keats

There is only one **happiness** in **life**, to love and be loved.

George Sand

Love is but the **discovery** of ourselves in others, and the delight of **recognition**.

Alexander Smith

But to **see** her was to love her, love
but her, and **love** her forever.

Robert Burns

To love is to receive a **glimpse**
of **heaven**.

Karen Sunde

A life without love is like a year
without **summer**.

Swedish proverb

A **caress** is better than a career.

Elisabeth Marburg

Each **moment** of a happy lover's hour is worth an **age** of dull and common life.

Aphra Behn

Love can turn the cottage into a **golden** palace.

German proverb

When the **heart** clings to a lover,
who **cares** what caste he be?

Indian proverb

When two **hearts** are one, even the **king** cannot separate them.

Turkish proverb

With you I should love to live, with you be ready to die.

Horace

Oh, what a dear **ravishing** thing
is the beginning of an **amour**!

Aphra Behn

Love doesn't just lay there, like a stone, it has to be made, like bread; re-made all the time, made new.

Ursula K. Le Guin

Love looks not with **eyes**, but with the **mind.**

William Shakespeare

Love must **blossom.**
Through **love** will grow the
trees and the bushes.

Joost van der Vondel

There is a name **hidden** in the shadow of my soul, where I read it **night** and day and no other eye sees it.

Alphonse de Lamartine

You had my **heart**, and I yours; a heart for a heart, good fortune for good **fortune**.

Marcelline Desbordes-Valmore

You are the prisoner of my heart;

the key is lost.

Old German song

Love guides the **stars** towards each other, the world plan endures only through love.

J. C. F. von Schiller

One **glance**, one word from you gives more pleasure than all the **wisdom** of this world.

J. W. von Goethe

Love and the gentle **heart** are but the same thing.

Dante

Let your heart **melt** toward me, just

as the ice that melts in **spring**
leaves no trace of its chill.

Kokin Shu

He who shall never be divided from me **kissed** my mouth all **trembling**.

Dante

love letters

'That's rather a sudden pull up, ain't it, Sammy?' inquired Mr Weller.

'Not a bit on it,' said Sam; 'she'll vish there wos more, and that's the great art o' letter writin'.'

Charles Dickens, *The Pickwick Papers*

Can no honest man have a prepo[sse]ssion for a fine woman, but he must run his head against an intrigue? Take a little of the tender witchcraft of Love, and add it to the generous, the honorable sentiments of manly friendship, and I know but one more friendly morsel, which few, few in any rank ever taste. Such a composition is like adding cream to the strawberries: it not only gives the fruit a more elegant richness, but has a peculiar deliciousness of its own.

Robert Burns to Clarinda (Agnes MacLehose), 1787

You will understand that I should like to say many fine and striking things to you, but it is rather difficult, all at once, in this way. I regret this all the more as you are sufficiently great to inspire one with romantic dreams of becoming the confidant of your beautiful soul...

Marie Bashkirtseff to Guy de Maupassant, 1884

If you only knew how much I love you, how essential you are to my life, you would not dare stay away for an instant, you would always remain pressed close to my heart, your soul to my soul.

Juliette Drouet to Victor Hugo, 1833

To me you are the gate of paradise. For you I will renounce fame, creativity, everything. Fidelina, Fidelina – I long for you intensely and frightfully.

Frederic Chopin to Delphine Potocka, 1835

My heart overflows with emotion and joy! I do not know what heavenly languor, what infinite pleasure permeates it and burns me up. It is as if I had never loved!!! Tell me whence these uncanny disturbances springs, these inexpressible foretastes of delight, these divine tremors of love.

Franz Liszt to Marie d'Agoult, 1834

Dearest, – I wish I had the gift of making rhymes, for methinks there is poetry in my head and heart since I have been in love with you. You are a poem. You are a sort of sweet, simple, gay, pathetic ballad, which Nature is singing, sometimes with tears, sometimes with smiles, and sometimes intermingled smiles and tears.

Nathaniel Hawthorne to Sophie Hawthorne, 1839

You fear, sometimes, I do not love you so much as you wish? My dear girl I love you ever and ever and without reserve. The more I have known you the more have I lov'd. In every way - even my jealousies have been agonies of love, in the hottest fit I ever had I would have died for you.

The last of your kisses was ever the sweetest; the last smile the brightest; the last movement the gracefullest. When you pass'd my window home yesterday, I was fill'd with as much admiration as if I had then seen you for the first time.

John Keats to Fanny Brawne, 1820

So many contradictions, so many contrary movements are true, and can be explained in three words: I love you.

Julie de L'Espinasse to Hippolyte de Guibert, 1774

I have not spent a day without loving you; I have not spent a night without embracing you; I have not so much as drunk a cup of tea without cursing the pride and ambition which force me to remain separated from the moving spirit of my life.

Napoleon Bonaparte to Josephine Bonaparte, 1796

You know I would with pleasure give up all here and all beyond the grave for you, and in refraining from this, must my motives be misunderstood? I care not who knows this, what use is made of it – it is you and to you only that they owe yourself.

I was and am yours freely and most entirely, to obey, to honour, love – and fly with you when, where, and how you yourself might and may determine.

Lord Byron to Lady Caroline Lamb, 1812

Love does not lie only in gazing towards each other, but it is looking into our future together, with four eyes, I think this is the test of our love.

Gopal Puri to Kailash Puri, 1942

You never knew, or never will know the very big and devastating love I had for you. How I adored every hair, every curl on your beard. How I devoured you whilst you read to me at night. How I loved the smell of your face in your sponge. Then the ivory skin on your hands, your voice, and your hat when I saw it coming along the top of the garden wall from the window.

(Dora) Carrington to Lytton Strachey, 1921

No heart ever wished another more truly 'many happy returns'; or if 'happy returns' are not in our vocabulary then 'wise returns', wise and true and brave, which after all are the only 'happiness', as I conjecture, that we have any right to look for in this segment of Eternity that we are traversing together, thou and I. God bless thee, Darling; and know thou always, in spite of the chimeras and delusions that thou art dearer to me than any earthly creature.

Thomas Carlyle to Jane Welsh Carlyle, 1846

It joys me to hear thy soul prospereth; the Lord increase His favours to thee more and more. The great good thy soul can wish is, That the Lord lift upon thee the light of His countenance, which is better than life. The Lord bless all thy good counsel and example to all those about thee, and hear all thy prayers, and accept thee always.

Oliver Cromwell to Elizabeth Cromwell, 1651

Classic Love Poems

£9.99
Hardback

Classic Love Poems contains a cross section of the true 'classics' of the genre, and constitutes a thorough representation of the enduring power of love over all humankind.

Poets in this anthology include: Blake, Byron, Chaucer, Coleridge, Donne, Keats, Marlowe, Marvell, Milton and many others.

Chocoheaven

£4.99
PPC

To err is human, to eat chocolate is divine.

This is the ultimate treat for chocolate lovers: with the history of the food of the gods to choco-myths and famous chocoholics; with choco-horoscopes, choco-games and choco-recipes. So go on, tear off the wrapper and indulge in *Chocoheaven* …

www.summersdale.com